The Love Notes

Mario Givens

The Love Notes

Copyright © 2017 by Mario Givens

All rights reserved. No part of this book may be reproduced or transmitted in any form or by any means without written permission from the author.

ISBN-13: 978-0-692-83786-3

Printed in the United States of America

Foreword

Author Mario Givens has a way with words like no other, his style is unique, calm, and vibrant, grasping a new way of delivering the content of poetry with love and caring.

Each chapter is written to connect an audience whose mind has no barriers no limits and open to an eternity of ideas that are geared to attach itself to your soul.

May this book "The Love Notes" leave you speechless and embraced with a message of love.

Acknowledgments

Writing a Book is a very challenging obstacle and I'm so grateful for a lot of people who dedicated their time to motivate me, inspire me, and support me throughout the process. To acknowledge your love ones is important because we all win when one is successful in the journey of writing a book. I want to thank god for giving me the ability to write and create visions with words.

I want to thank my immediate family Elisha, Nia, Mario jr because it was a battle to finish this book with so much going on in my life now writing this book and they brought the fire in me out. To know you have people there to help guide you with their love makes the book sweeter for me. This book is dedicated to them and I want to leave this book to my children so they can have some motivation to make them see dreams do come true.

Dedication

I want to thank my mom, grandma, sisters and brothers RIP Markie. I want to thank all my family and friends who is all over the country that supported me. I want to thank Tiffany Green, Jordan Rivers for their efforts in making this book a success and dealing with my demanding ways to get it done thank you both.

I want to send a big shout out to Paul L. Dunbar high school alumni and especially class of 96 for always giving me love and support; Go mighty men and mighty women.

Introduction

The Love Notes is a written expression, created to take you on a journey as far as your imagination allows. The heart of this creation uses symbolism, as a definition, an art of love. Many poems in this book comes from real life events and all poems are written and arrange by me the author.

Contents

Foreword iii
Acknowledgments iv
Dedication v
Introduction vi
It's Perfection 1
Solar Love 2
Silent Whispers 3
Talking to the moon 4
Red Tears 6
White Rose 7
God Chose Me 9
Black Rose 10
Found You 12
The Good Times 13
A Letter to You 14
Stormy Weather 15
A Death of a Butterfly 16
Your Spiritual Scent 17
My Vow to You 18
A Mental Picnic with You 20
Thoughts of a beautiful Ancestor 22
That Kiss 23
The End of Royalty 25
Butterfly 26
Response from the Sun 27
One Tear 29

Inspiring Friendship	30
A Day Dream Date	31
Chapter Completed	32
Sincerity	34
Red wine	35
Daydream	36
Quiet Tears	38
A Royal thought	39
Spiritual dove	40
A special day	42
Reconstruction of love	44
Lady bug	46
Punctuation of love	48
Beauty	49
A complicated dream	51
A short thought	53
Glance	54
When a man loves	55
My Gift	57
No tears	59
It's not a dream	61
Blessings from God	63
A moment of hope	65
Patient to make love	67
Mrs class	69
A race to win a heart	71
About the Poet	73

Mario Givens

It's Perfection

We may seem distant It's Perfection
The moon kisses the sun
Her glare is the warmth she gives me in the night
My rays are the smile because she supports my blessings
I commend her submission
A good deed
It's like a peaceful ride on a horse
Traveling to heaven
It's perfection
Dedication
I'm honored to consider those eyes
Humble
This god surprise
I'll kneel tonight with gratefulness
Sincere
A dream
No need to pinch
I don't want to wake from this kiss

Solar Love

Sitting here
My mind is alone like the moon glaring at earth
Wondering
Wishing
Hoping
Even prayed
Whatever do it mean
Why can't my universe connect to her planet?
Spiritual love making
Endless hearts taken
Just can't understand
Can't comprehend
Emotionally confuse
A future kingdom
Has no royalty
The crowns have no heads
What can I do?
What can I say?
Guess all I can do
Is be patient, believe, trust, and pray.

Silent Whispers

I'm lost
My tears create puddles
A heart that needs healing
Broken feelings
The only cure is you
The antidote to a running cupid
I miss you
That moment where I can hear your voice
The sacred words
The medicine to my pain
I need you
Comeback
I'm devastated
I just want that fire
The opportunity to show change
Write a love story with my kiss
I want to be motivated by your inspiration
I want to feel safe
My security
Hearing you say I love you.

Talking to the Moon

When I See You My Nights Get Brighter
My Mood Gets to The Point Where I'm Happy
You Keep Me at Peace
At the Point in My Life My Mind Is at Ease
You Have This Glow When I Look at You
It's Like You Are Telling Me Something
The Good and The Bad
The Advice I Need
Why You Don't Speak to Me
Why I must Speculate
Wondering If You Think.
This Relationship Is Hard
Sometimes I Feel Like Giving Up
I Trust You
I Love You
Every morning When I See You
I Need You
You Are So Distant from Me
I Can't Hold You
Put My Arms Around You
It Hurts Because There's Not a Night I'm Not Around You
I Know Others Feel the Same Way
Just Don't Cheat Me Out of My Peace

I'll Stay in My Place
I'll Become Submissive
Until the Next Time You Put a Smile on My Face.

Red Tears

It hurts
It brings the sad in me
The bad that I want to do
The negative love inside me that's true
All I do is cry
Let my tears bleed pain down my cheek
My mind is so deep
I feel like dying
Go into this lifetime sleep
Where I dream
These situation is too much
The silent screams
The quiet yells
That has my soul possessed
Is it demons I guess
The blood in my eyes
Takes my pain on a date
It hurts so bad
The water dries from the sadness in my face
I need to find a way out
Take a trip to smiles
Take a vacation from this situation
So, my tears can be clear.

White Rose

White rose
You are the same
So, bright and pure
Don't ever change
Leave your pedals on my floor
So, I can take that trip right to your glow.
White rose
Smells like that summer day
The scent of perfume
That gets all in my way
The stem so strong
When I try to hold you I can't let go
Your roots are your love
Your heart is all the things that this man wants.
White rose
The wind blew you back in my world
I want to water you
So eventually you will be my girl
The thought of you makes my mind goes into a twirl
Makes me think I want you mine
Need your foundation as you blossom to my side.
I want to be that bee and that humming bird to your soul
Have our evolution create one mold?

One garden can create many different flowers
These extra plants and the fertilizer will be us making love.

God Chose Me

He saw more than dirt
My skin has worth
He saw greatness when he made me
A sculpture of hope
My eyes were his frames of love
My mouth was the prophecy that was told
From the fingers that holds faith
A heart that beats inspiration
My soul has spirit
I have purpose
An angel of motivation
It was written.

Black Rose

From a distant
I can smell your scent
The kind of smell
Only god can send
So sweet
Very warm with class
The perfect scenery
My heartbeat performs fast
When I look at the moon
I see your smile
A wink at the sun
Peaceful as the clouds
I look for you
The garden is empty
I guess someone pick you
After you blossom without me
Where are you
The smile is here
The love in my soul
Eyes full of tears
Whenever you need me to water your roots
Grow into my garden
I'll know what to do

Mario Givens

> I'll put you in a vase
> So, the world will see
> The rose of my world
> Your beauty I will showcase.

Found You

I can't believe I found you
standing in plain view
had my heart pumping emotions
I still can't believe it's true.
My dream came to reality
I pinch myself to make sure
your eyes conquer me
I didn't know what to do
You were standing there
like the only rose left
I had to try again
Your heart I should've kept.

The Good Times

You are my soul mate
The person I can't live without
No matter where you at
Listen to my inner thoughts shout.
It's like a wake dream with a lot to see
Pictures from the past
Do you think it was meant to be?
If only you will give me a chance
To express myself with a little romance
When you left, the dream was clear
A strange nightmare without you here
Our love is like a chapter
Let's turn the page
To a better relationship
That shouldn't begin with rage
If I could turn back the hands of time
Let's get one thing clear
In my heart, I knew I believe in faith.

A Letter to You

Our hearts are close
The blood is our togetherness
Our souls are what we love the most.
No need for sorry, I truly understand
We may shed tears for our feelings
Always remember you are a man.
Stay positive through your journey of time
Focus on your goal
Eventually freedom you will find.
The next time you kneeled and pray to the lord
Ask him for the strength you will need
These tears are from me to you
Always keep me in your heart
I do truly miss and love you.

Stormy Weather

Where are you
missing in action
how you could leave
I guess you couldn't remember me.
Come back
I need you
what more can I do
bring back the memories
my love for you is true
Beyond the clouds is where I want to take you
so, when we make love
our bodies can collide and make a storm.
My heart is the thunder that pounds your soul
the wetness from your body is the rain that pours
My strong ejaculation erupts your human volcano
the hot relaxing lava warms my outer thoughts.
Let me hold your hand
kiss below your wrist
true love is not hard to find
your love I really miss.

A Death of a Butterfly

A sad day
The air is very thin
As it blows my way
The tears are emotional
Uncontrollable
The flower dies
As the sky cries
The ground is fill with tears
Why this happen
No answers
It's just a long day
A death of a butterfly
The rainbow has no colors
The peace becomes chaos
Smiles are frowns
The clouds are dark
Lakes are dry
Bees refuse to buzz
Nightmares are dreams
Agitated by the autopsy of love.

Your Spiritual Scent

Natural Scent
The flowers had envy
So, they wither
Your scent blows
Every time the wind talks
I can smell it
Indulge in your heart
It's like a rose
Just one
Because you are one of a kind
Scared
Special
No vase is worth your presence
Only the Garden of Eden
Can be the place
For your Forever Scent.

My Vow to You

My vow to you is true, the consistency of my love is
Faithful, and I will never lie to you.

My feelings plus your feelings equals forever
Situations may get bad, as long as we are together
our lives will continue to get better.

My vow to you is true, there's days I have no clue
As long as you are by my side, the other days I will know
what to do.

The kneeled down proposal I present in front of you
a lifetime commitment, I want to share my heart and
Soul with you.

This promise I made will never be broken,
to have a woman like you, you are my infinite token.

My deepest desires may burn when you aren't around.
I look at the longevity of love, I present you with the royal
crown.

My vow to you is true, if the sky continues to be blue;

    the faithfulness of my mind and the desire in me
        Heart, my soul will always love you.

A Mental Picnic with You

A secluded place
Only my mind is the basket
It has all the food
Love
Life
Goals
A menu of truth
Just don't know what to do
So, I lay it all out on my mental table
Pour a sip of peace
As you taste it
You at ease
Feed your humbleness
As I watch you become happy
The wind is clear
The sun is near
The lake has a sound
The birds sing I love you with every chirp

The flowers scent has nothing on you
Then I woke up and just see your face
　　　A mental picnic with you.

Thoughts of a Beautiful Ancestor

So, beautiful
Like the sun during the day
She's the moon contacting the stars
Then she requests love
Her strength
I can hold her in my dreams
Making love to her screams
She penetrates my heart with her eyes
Went deep inside my soul
She's modest
I can relax my head on her ideas
Let my reasons expand to her truth
I want to release my passion into her world
I depend on her
The backbone of my life
I will protect my emotions with her spiritual sword.

That Kiss

It was warm
A feeling that calms a storm
Her kiss
So, Warm
A night I truly will miss
That kiss
That keeps the romance near my heart
A sensual feeling
An internal spark
That kiss again
I can't stop thinking
My eyes open
As my inner thoughts begin to speak
That kiss
That had my lower part
Reaching its peak
An embrace
Lips on that soft face
Look in my eyes
You wanted me to stay in your space
A kiss
That can slow the fast
So, elegant

The Love Notes

Thinking about what's next
All this over that kiss
A memory of love
With a moment, I truly miss.

Mario Givens

The End of Royalty

A kingdom without a king
A queen without her crown
A princess with tears
A prince with a lifetime frown
The world of pain
An internal soul
Hearts of shame
A vision of happiness
Now eyes that's close
Nothing to see
Just thoughts to unfold
The passion has dies
The love has tears
That drains from the eyes
Forever was too far
Only chosen ones get to go
It's like a little taste of heaven
A love with an everlasting glow
Great things come to an end
I'll take the good out of it all
So ill have memories
The pleasant ones
As a kingdom of love falls.

Butterfly

Too many colors
like a rainbow across the sky
lightening up the darkness
your essence is not a surprise
I see you everyday
I'm starting to fall in love
sometimes I wave at you
your flight is more flawless than a dove
I miss you in the winter
I guess you could just like me
when the spring and summer comes
I notice our relationship begins
I'm glad you are back
in the winter, do you cheat
because when the season changes
you get so bright to me.
I'll never hurt you
that's a fight I do not need
I let you fly across my life
with that exotic and peaceful speed.

Response from the Sun

I Understand
Everything Will Be Okay
You Bring Shine to Me
Your Hair Is Your Glow from Your Rays
Please Know I Do Care
Truthfully, I Feel You the One
Honestly You Are My Soul
You Are So Hot
Sometimes I Wish You Were Cold
Every day When I Wake
I Look for You
I Stare into Your Light
Wishing I Could Be Your Energy
That Keep You at The Highest Point in Your Life
You Right
I Believe in Your Thoughts
I See Why You Just Here
Trying to Keep Me Warm and Pure with Water
I Know You Mad When I Look Elsewhere
Talking to The Moon

Letting Her Know How I Feel
How My Life Should Be
We Will Discuss Our Love When I Wake and Look for You.

One Tear

One tear
The kind that cries
Worries
Many questions whys
A sad moment
What is he thinking
A mind full of thoughts
A world is sinking
Many dreams
These words
I hear over and over
Scared of truth
Honesty don't live here
This can't happen to me
All the things I fear
Why this one tear
It has many reasons
No happiness
A negative season
The pain is wet
It drops out of one eye
While the other eye is confusing
One side of me dies
As the other side, won't cry

Inspiring Friendship

You are my support
Saw my vision
Executed my mission
My goal was true
My heart was real
I know what to do
My mind adopted you
My soul honored you
You are my friend
A lifetime token
The reasons I smile
The loyalty
The respect I have for you
The praise of sacredness
I will forever love.

A Day Dream Date

A stare
Thinking about this feeling about this woman
Should I give her a chance?
A night of romance
The ability to create a feeling for this man
I want her to understand
I know my worth
I have a lot to give
More than she knows
A perfect night
A walk inside my mental park
Where the trees speak to the grass
As we pass
I just want more
The opportunity to see her smile
I want the world to experience her shine
The sun has no brightness
I will appreciate and cherish that night
Her took her rays
When I kiss her goodnight.

Chapter Completed

It started as a dream
A goal
A wonderful thought of forever
A moment to visualized the word love
The happiness
The ability to make another feels safe
Warm
Secured within themselves
Motivation creates inspiration
A breath of fresh air
Someone who cares
The making of a legacy
She brings out the best in me
The fire that desire the moments of calm
The responsibility to be free
An angel in flight
A heart soft like the clouds on a sunny day
It's like a peaceful pray
God guides her love to kiss my hate
So, I congratulate
Appreciate
Cherish the opportunity to be on a throne
Holding hands from a spiritual home

Crowns that sits on a shelf of confusion
A page that ends after a period from a sentence
The love decided to leave
Another chapter completed.

Sincerity

I am me

A man

A mistake that comes with lessons

Strong

The support of a system no one can change

Humble

Giving others joy from my heart

Grateful

Believes that my spirit is my foundation

Dedicated

Putting my all into my purpose

Rejuvenated

Finding peace inside my mind

Inspired

The ability to accept criticism and apply it

Motivated

Responsible for allowing guidance to subdued me

Genuine

Only I can execute gods plans for me

Complete

Understanding it was written and I read the story.

Red wine

A sip of perfection
Ingredients that soothes the soul
The taste of patience
A relaxing feeling
It's like a comfort zone
A quiet home
Words of wisdom
A vacation from stress
A peaceful vision
It's an opportunity to be at ease

Daydream

As she stares into my eyes
My heartbeat has paused
What's the caused
I'm poise for the reasoning
Wishing this dream was a reality
I decided to sleep in
Continue to love
Enjoy the romance
All from a glance
Her voice sings
Every word to my ears
She communicates with peace
Leaving me at ease
A whisper of ecstasy
She seduces my emotions
So, beautiful
The sun is jealous
The moon makes love to my secrets
I want a kiss
Forever peck

Mario Givens

I sincerely miss
When my eyes open
I want to lay my eyes to sleep
Hoping she invites her heart
To my dreams

Quiet Tears

A sense of silence
Only cries are inside my eye lids
The pain I endure, the world won't know
So, I carry it on my sleeves
It stung like a vicious bee
But I created this honey
Whereas my attack came from the hive
My feelings I won't hide
But I'll get my emotions back in check
my heart was broke
You may think it's not that serious
What we discuss wasn't a joke
my heart is not in a laughing mood
My spirit doesn't think it's funny
I'm glad you happy
Deceit is not home
I will always love you
The love is gone.

A Royal Thought

In my thoughts
I'm guided by wishes and hopes
Finding myself anxious
Meditating to cope
She always captures my eyes
What do you see?
A Queen
Her crown controls my heart
Submissive to her words
I kneeled before her
Kiss her hand and feet
Then I bow to her
Letting her know she can trust me
But the distance between her throne and mines
Keeps the kingdom silent
But I feel her energy
Producing waves in my chakras
I'm control by the universe.

Spiritual Dove

The ability to be the standard
A dove takes her landing
You are beautiful
The moon is your smile
The lake shadows that smile
Your heart is the rays of the night
You are kind
Your spirit is measure by your character
You are defining by sincerity
Confidence is your stability
You know your worth
It's the opportunity to love
The ability to make me better
As I sit and think
It was you
The one who speaks volumes to my heart
Tells him I love you
Secures me with every beat
That smiles creates an energy
It's call Peace
The tip of the iceberg
The plateau of love
The hills of modesty

Mario Givens

That comes from A spiritual dove

A Special Day

The grass
Is where I lay
Thinking
Hoping
Praying for you
the breeze soothes my soul
Creates a guard
From the cold heart
I can hear the ocean
Telling me you still care
That our love was rare
So, sacred to the truth
As the sea gulls flew
Telling me this what I should do
Take your hand
Consider your eyes
These Feelings that can't be disguise.
Take a walk
Enjoy the sand through our toes
Who knows
What the fish may think
What the whales would say
As the dolphins play

Mario Givens

The sun winks with praise
Picking up rocks
Take a short throw
They skip across the water
Just Like your soul skips
My heart is like the wind
Got the leaves cheering
God creations
Enjoying our special day.

Reconstruction of Love

It was a cold day
The whispers come from the echoes
A shallow creek
The whispers are closer
It seems desperate
Agitated from the thoughts of concerns
A soul burns
Caught in a fire of destruction
The construction
The road blocks
Where was the speed bumps?
Speeds of emotions
No internal red light to stop
Yellow makes me Think
Caution for the next pedestrian
An intersection of choices
Rush hour begins
A traffic jam of hearts
Stuck behind love
In front of me is lust
Temptation waves to the left

Mario Givens

Only way to go is right
A detour to Home
Now I have a piece of mind.

Lady Bug

She stood there patiently
Waiting for my touch
Her eyes launch love my way
I accept with confidence
Still not knowing what to say
So, beautiful
Amazing and full of grace
She's dress so modestly
Orange and black
We connect
Just me and her
Communicating
Rhythms and waves
Our energy
Produces chemistry
Creates opportunity
Her smile
My smile
Evolution of love
The sun jealous because she has a shine
What is she thinking?
What's on her mind?
It seems like time stopped

Like days made love to nights
The moon put the stars to sleep
The calmness of her aura
Sort of like she's shy
I don't want this to end
It's so peaceful
Like a warm hug
A long conversation with a
Lady bug

Punctuation of Love

She knows
I sent the words
I express the verbs
Created many verses
Use commas to add how I feel
Question marks to wonder why
Quotations so she knows I'm honest
Exclamation points when I'm excited about her
I wrote so much
Because I love her so much
That it hurts
God this is who I want
Who I need
What more do I have to do
Do I deserve her?
Worthy of her
She's my book
My chapters
Paragraph of love
She keeps breaking my heart
She ends it with a period.

Beauty

It's was a dream
opportunity knocks at my heart
a silent voice says her peace
I'm here for you
I come to make things true
I still couldn't see her
I knew it was an angel
her wings rub my face
my heart beats at a rapid pace
I'm at ease
When she looks at me
She had a face of grace
she's everything I wanted so far
I decided to kneeled
Giving the creator praised
I'm bless and I deserve this woman
You should see this woman
She has an angelic face
perfection in her smile
A goddess with an inspirational voice
She demands respect
Only a gentleman understands

A vision of love
She has eyes of a keen eagle
As she takes flight up above.

Mario Givens

A Complicated Dream

I was anxious and nervous
But I kept my composure
I always wanted to be with her
The thoughts
My arms wrap around her
It felt like royalty
A moment where a King meets a Queen
Her wings grasp my Halo
Heaven was the flash from the camera
Picture perfect
My internal smile
Seems like the moon
Smiles at the lake
Mentally in a great place
But I never stop hoping
Wishing, thinking, anticipating
The moments being near her
It Was like flowers in Gods garden
My eyes romance hers
I pray one day I could hear her voice

A beautiful Choice
Then the phone rung
I believe it was her
Until I realize my dream was a nightmare
When I wipe my eyes
Knowing I was kiss in my sleep by an angel

Mario Givens

A Short Thought

It was like a classic movie
I took you on a date
Walk you down the beach
As you listen to the words I say
You are on my mind
Why did you cross my thoughts?
I'm Trying to remind speechless
So, I stay quiet
Don't want rejection to conquer my heart
But I continue to be true
Staying humble
Grateful that I talk to you
It's like peace through words
My body melts
When I see your face
It Puts me in another place
Like Venus
The planet of love
maybe a star
It shoots above
Lands inside a thought
A sacred moment
When she opens my heart.

Glance

It's your eyes
I cherish your thoughts
I can see your love
When I glare
Don't mean to stare
I'm so amuse buy your lioness
So, I need to caress
Put my emotions through my veins
So, it can contact to your soul
I smile next to you
I know I'm safe
Put away in your scared jail
More than a around a way girl
You more like the queen
Who demands respect
So, glad we met
Accomplish moments
A classic token
So, I thank you

When a Man Loves

The ability to lead
A protector of his home
He guides the soul
His first piece of gold
He desires your heart
When he kisses your lips
His eyes are dark
He's at peace with your pleasure
He tries to conceal his treasure
Nobody can have this gem
I'll wear your love on my neck
My forever charm
This love is so strong
Trying to satisfy, But his dedication
Will not be overlooked
His hard work
The abilities to play his part
He has loyalty and will fight to the end
His love comes out of his pores
A lifetime friend

He's the anchor
The motivator and the caretaker
He's what every woman needs
The husband
The man who will do whatever it takes
When he makes love to you
Your body feels like a vacation
You so relax
He conquers your world
That your planets become one earth
He's so sincere
His words become sentences
You have many chapters
The author of my thoughts
I want to publish this love
Inside a special woman heart

Mario Givens

My Gift

Is it the opportunity that evolves?
With happiness
The bundle of joy that once had you cry
Because of her eyes
It's call love
The ability to make a woman become a mother
The earth produces a garden with one rose
You cherish the seed you planted
God is proud
The same god that put the joy back in your life
You sadden days are gone
Your chance to feel safe
Kennedy secures your soul
But brace yourself
She maybe the little girl that runs around and take your world to the heavens
There's days where she will grow up
Leave the nest
What will you do?
How could you let her go?
But she's still close to your heart
Memories that will spark
That will take you back to the start

The Love Notes

And you will realize
You did your part
The love of a child
Another successful girl
That will become a woman

Mario Givens

No Tears

My cries create puddles
Visions of hurt
Explanations of pain
I surrender to reasoning
My eyes need a vacation
A peaceful sight of love
Emotions have confusion
Mental breakdown
Umbrellas
Shelters
The rain pours the soul
The pain
The forecast says hurt
The sun escapes his duty
It's gloomy
The clouds lose its worth
The rain started as a drizzle
Ended as a flood
It will take days to clear
All from one tear
The inability to conquer fear
The storm hasn't pass
The thunder pounds

Leaving a heart attack
As my emotions and spirit clash
All from one word
The same word that haunts
Strikes
Rips the internal
A mental inferno
Eyes burn
My Thoughts mourn
All from a thought of failing

Mario Givens

It's Not a Dream

They do exist
But you can't resist
The inability to be yourself
Stops your opportunities
So, there's no knock
Only answer you got was sadness
Because you passive
You can't speak
Only your inner voice speaks
I can't hear
So, I move on
Then I turn around
Only Your fears
Stops your security
But we connect through thoughts
I need more
You need more
My heart is my soul
A break can tear a spirit
So, comfort my words
I will caress your nouns
But I still need more
You still need more

I want to hold your hand
Express my silence through clouds
Your head is on my shoulder, the stars is shining
We are day and night
But our universe is missing
We are forever
When the sun makes love to the moon.

Blessings from God

A moment
I realize that dreams may come true
Only a sheep jumps across my bed
The moon shines
The lake has a glow
It's the clouds at night
As the waves flow
Her smile
It makes the sun jealous
The sun decides to set west
Take a rest to allow the Angels to fly
She's a verse from a scripture I once read
The birds sing
The sounds of horns that plays Gods song
It's call Her Beauty
My duty is to serenade her
Cherish, Respect, and love her
To whereas I motivate her
I will direct her
Lead her to water

The Love Notes

she will drink first
Not a love curse
This is passion
Romance from my heart
God gave me permission
I submit to her soul
We are face to face
No words
Just a modest stare
Perfection
I may be missing a rib
She accepts the roses I brought
I whisper my feelings
Your eyes are Gods thoughts.

Mario Givens

A Moment of Hope

Have you ever wanted to make love to someone so bad?
It's an ultimate thought that crashes your visions
I want to read her body like a scripture
A perfect picture
Because your frame is the ultimate art work
Self-worth
The ability to make a man pray
That one day He can give you his energy
Make your body explode with passion
From his desires
Your land pours out a soothing lake
Relaxing moment at the bay
Where Patience meets wait
that thought is a perfect view
A piece to the puzzle
The missing clue
I never was a fan of day dreaming
But when I wonder off into my thoughts
I see you
Feel you
Kiss you
Hear you
But what a man supposed to do?

The Love Notes

The next time to see you
I'll express my love for you

Patient to Make Love

I waited
Anticipated
The thoughts of me putting my love inside you
So, when you release your energy
My connection is positive
But I got more to give
Secure my emotions
So, I won't confuse love from lust
I injected my trust
You receive a dosage
That way every ejaculation has a meaning
A purpose
Longevity
Souls surface
The Earth moves
Many Clouds pause
Rain pours
I must give more
I want to Create a fire
Eliminate a desire

implement a need
So, the want is minimum
Every touch is passionate
Not venom
You can look inside my eyes
The words I love you
Will thrust
When God allow the earth to beat.

Mrs. Class

I saw her
She was by the river
Looking at the fish
With a smile
It was like the sun
The water was calm
The birds chirp
The wind blew a cool breeze
The branches shiver
A slow walk across the leaves
She's like autumn
A quiet moment
A second to think
As she stands
With her nice dress
Shoes to match her charm
Elegance
She's a page of grace
Beauty
Like the bird that flew pass
A smirk on her face
She knows she's great
Confident

Pride
Modesty as she stands in her place
A woman knows her worth
She dug deep inside her purse
She pulls out her honesty
Painted her lips with loyalty
Put makeup of love on her cheeks
Her eye liner was a vision of God
she combs her hair of trust
Before she takes a stroll of peace
She bends over and sincerity ties the shoes on her feet

A Race to Win a Heart

I wanted many dreams to come true
First day I laid eyes
I knew it could be you
So, I ask God can he lead me
Take the baton of Love
Pass it to my heart
So, I can run faster to get to you
The finish line is us making love forever
I hear the whispers in the air
The wind telling me you are
True, loyal, caring, and secure
I continue to run harder
The birds chirp words as I run pass
She has the qualities of a Queen
Spirit of a Goddess
Elimination of her past
I can see the finish line
It's far but so close because
Respect
Honor

Gratitude

Sincerity I got for her
Is the strength in my spine?
I'm in front of them all
My sweat is the crave I have for her
The tightness of my muscles will be worth the lifetime massage she gives me
The vision is the time shared
She's worth the future of romance
Hopefully God understand
That's why I want to win her forever

About the Poet

Mario Givens is a native of Chicago. The artist of this creative work, "The Love Notes". His accomplishments include a degree in Criminal Justice, a community activist, a high school baseball coach, and a juvenile mentor. Clearly his purpose exceeds this productive literary piece. Mario enjoys pouring his heart into charity work and strives to make a difference with his unique character and mindset. Stay tuned, greater works will be expedited from his world of poetry.

For Booking Contact
773-627-7175
Mariogivens@yahoo.com